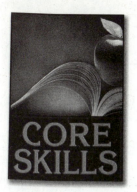

GRADE
1

Social Studies

ISBN-13: 978-1-4190-3423-7

Steck-Vaughn is a trademark of Harcourt Achieve Inc.

The paper used in this book comes from sustainable resources.

Printed in the United States of America.
3 4 5 6 7 8   1413   14 13 12 11 10
4500224655

Steck Vaughn™

A Harcourt Achieve Imprint

www.HarcourtSchoolSupply.com

Contents

Introduction

Social studies focuses on developing knowledge and skill in history, geography, culture, economics, civics, and government. It also focuses on people and their interaction with each other and the world in which they live. *Core Skills: Social Studies* addresses these areas of study and correlates with social studies curriculum throughout the United States. With this book, students can:

- gain a better understanding of their family and neighborhood
- practice map and geography skills
- work with charts and other graphic devices

The book features 12 chapter lessons on a variety of social studies topics. It also includes:

- special features such as "Around the World" and "Special People"
- interactive questions about the text or pictures
- a unit project to expand student involvement with the topics
- chapter checkups
- unit tests

Unit  1
FAMILIES

People live in families.
Families are alike and different.
- How are they alike?
- How are they different?

Unit Project

Cut out pictures of families from magazines. Find pictures of small families and large families. Gather pictures of your family. What makes families alike and different?

CHAPTER 1 What Is a Family?

How big is your **family**?
Some families are large.
Some families are small.
Look at the pictures.

➤ **Circle the large family.**

Put a blue ✔ next to the small family.

Is your family large?
Is your family small?

➤ **Draw a picture of your family.**

Draw your picture here.

My Family

We need families.
Families help us.
Families give us love.

➤ **Look at the picture.**

Circle the person who is helping.

Who is being helped?

Draw a line under the person.

Who helps you?

Write your answer here.

_____

- - - - - - - - - - - - - - - - - - -

_____

- - - - - - - - - - - - - - - - - - -

_____

- - - - - - - - - - - - - - - - - - -

_____

Families help in many ways.
They give us homes.
They give us clothes.
They give us food.

➤ **Look at each picture.**

Who is buying food?

Put a red ✔ next to the picture.

Who is making clothes?

Put a green ✔ next to the picture.

Families change.
Families get bigger.
Look at the pictures.
How has the family changed?

➤ **Which picture is the first taken of this family?**

Write <u>1</u> in the box.

Which picture comes next?

Write <u>2</u> in the box.

Which picture shows the family as it is now?

Write <u>3</u> in the box.

Families change in other ways, too.
Families move to new homes.
Adults in the family get new jobs.
Children go to new schools.

➤ **Look at each picture.**

Do the pictures show how a family changes?

Put a ✔ over the picture that shows change.

Unit Project **Tip!**

Ask your family for pictures.
Find pictures of your family having fun together.
Find pictures that show how your family has changed.
Put the pictures in a folder or book.

Gwendolyn Brooks

Special People

Gwendolyn Brooks was a poet.
She grew up in Chicago.
Gwendolyn never forgot what it was like growing up.
She wrote poems about it.
Some of her poems are about children and families.
Some poems are about things that families do.

➤ **What would you write about being in a family?**

Write your answer here.

_____

_____

_____

_____

_____

_____

_____

Unit 1, Chapter 1
Core Skills Social Studies 1, SV 9781419034237

Technology

Keeping in Touch

Families do not always live together. Families still want to know about each other.

➤ **Look at the pictures.**

How does your family keep in touch?

Put a ✔ next to ways your family uses.

Core Skills Social Studies 1, SV 9781419034237

Name _____   Date _____

Learning to Put Things in Order

➤ **Look at the pictures. Cindi is building something with her play logs.**

1. What happens first? Put a **1** in the box.

2. What happens next? Put a **2** in the box.

3. What happens next? Put a **3** in the box.

4. When has Cindi finished? Put a **4** in the box.

Chapter Checkup ✓

➤ **Look at the two pictures of the families below.**
Draw a line over the two oldest people in each family.
Put an X over the youngest person in each family.

Thinking & Writing

Tell one way families change.

Write your answer here.

_____

- -

_____

- -

_____

CHAPTER 2 Families Work and Play Together

Families work together.
They work at home.
Everyone can help.

➤ **Who is helping?**

Write your answer here.

_____
- -
_____
- -
_____

The boy is helping.
He can set the table.

➤ **How do you help?**

Write your answer here.

_____
- -
_____
- -
_____

Families play together.
They play at home and away.
They have fun.
Look at the pictures.

➤ **Put a ✔ on the family at home.**

Draw a line under the families having fun away from home.

Families have **rules**.
Rules tell us what to do and
what not to do.
Families have clean-up rules.
They have safety rules.

➤ **Look at the pictures.**

**What kind of rule does each
picture show?**

**Write your answer under each
picture.**

Unit Project

Tip!

Talk to your family about rules at home.
What rules do you have?
Think about why these rules are important.

Families have bedtime rules.
One rule is the hour we go to bed.
Another rule is to wash before bed.
We need rest to be healthy.

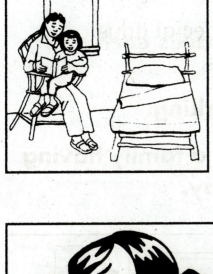

➤ **Read these rules.**

Put a ✔ next to some good bedtime rules.

Go to bed at a good hour. _____

_____

Play with your toys. _____

Eat a bad snack. _____

Brush your teeth. _____

Families Together

Families live in many places.
They live all around the world.
They work together.
They play together.
They have fun on special days.
Look at the pictures.

➤ **Circle a family working.**

Draw a line under a family having fun on a special day.

Chapter Activity

Learning About Near and Far

➤ **Look at the picture. Read the sentences. Do what they tell you to do.**

1. Find the children who are **near** the slide. Draw a line under them.

2. Which dog is **next to** the swings? Circle the dog.

3. Are the swings **near** or **far** from the dog you circled? Circle the answer.

   near   far

4. Is the slide **near** or **far** from the swings? Circle the answer.

   near   far

www.harcourtschoolsupply.com
21
Unit 1, Chapter 2
Core Skills Social Studies 1, SV 9781419034237

Chapter Checkup ✔

➤ **Look at the pictures.**

Draw a circle around each bike rider who is not following the rules.

 **Thinking & Writing**

Why do we need rules?
Write your answer here.

_____
- -
_____

_____

_____

22

Unit 1 ☐ Skill Builder

Understanding Alike and Different

Look at the pictures. Find the pictures that show how families are alike and different.

1. Families like to play in different ways. Circle the two families who are playing.

2. Families are alike because they work together. Draw a line between the two families who are working. How is their work different?

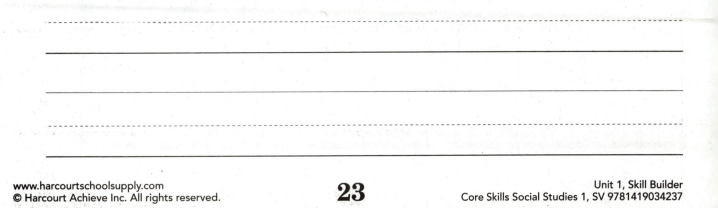

Present Your Project

Now it's time to finish your project. Talk about your ideas with your family or friends. Then answer these questions.

- **How are families alike?**

- **How are families different?**

- **How do families change?**

Try one of these ideas.

➤ Make a book called "Families Are Alike and Different." Use the pictures you found in magazines and the pictures you found at home. Talk about what is alike and different about families with your friends and family.

➤ Make a mural. Draw pictures of families having fun together at a picnic or in a park. Write the names of your family members on the mural.

Unit 1 ✏ Test

➤ **Look at the pictures.**

Does each picture show a family?

Write yes or no below each picture.

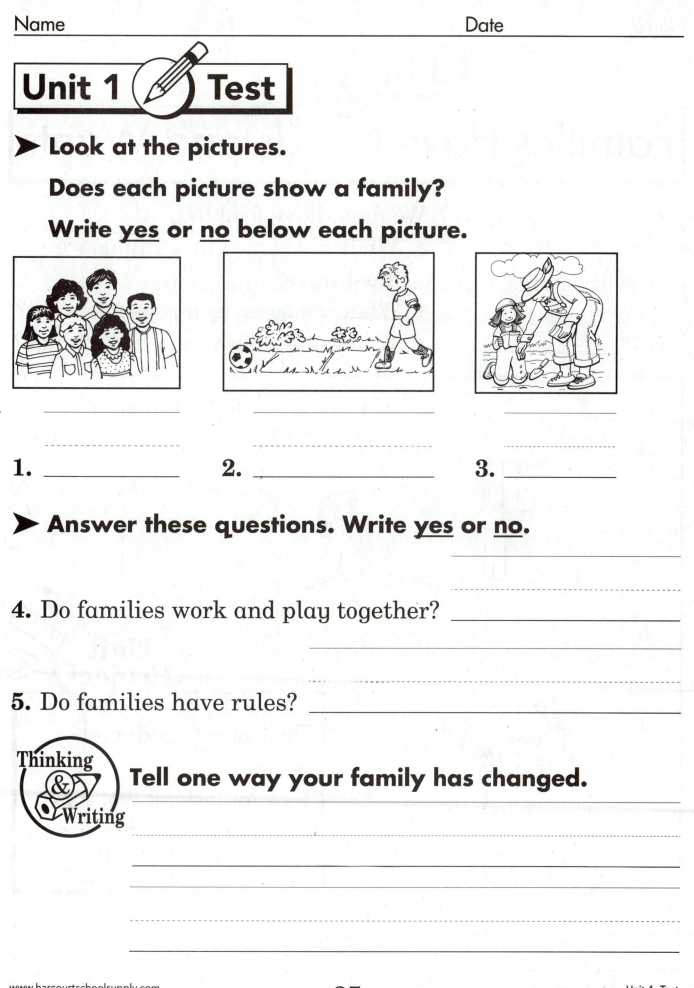

1. _____   2. _____   3. _____

➤ **Answer these questions. Write yes or no.**

4. Do families work and play together? _____

_____

5. Do families have rules? _____

Thinking & Writing Tell one way your family has changed.

_____

_____

_____

_____

Unit 2

Families Have Needs and Wants

We must have food to live.
- What are some other things we must have?
- What are some things people want?
- Who works to give us these things?

Unit Project

Think about needs and wants.
Look for pictures that show needs and wants families have.

CHAPTER 3 — What Do Families Need and Want?

Families need and want many things.
A **need** is something you must have to live.
A **want** is something you would like to have.

➤ **Look at the pictures.**

Draw a circle around needs.

Put a ✔ on wants.

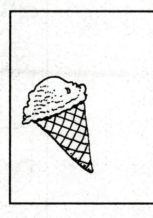

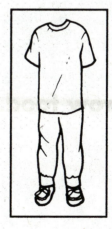

All families need food.
Families get food from different places.
We grow food.
We buy food.
We cook food.

➤ **Draw a line from each sentence to the picture it tells about.**

We buy food.

We grow food.

Families need homes.
Some homes are tall.
Some homes are small.
Some homes can be moved.
All homes keep us warm and dry.

➤ **Look at the pictures.**

Circle a tall home.

Draw a line under a home that can be moved.

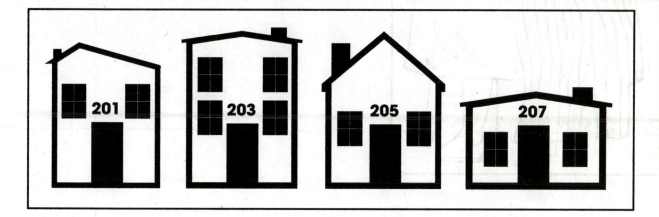

Families need clothing.
We buy clothes.
We make clothes.
We share clothes that are too small for us.

➤ **Look at the pictures.**

Circle someone who is buying clothes.

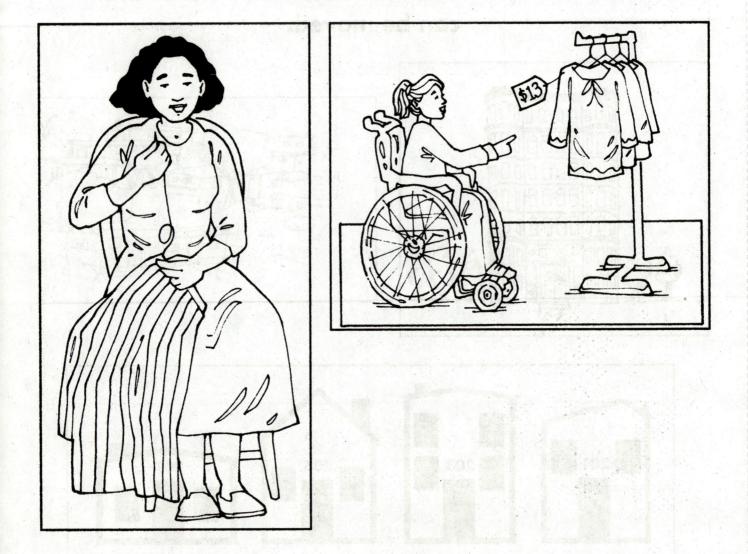

Families have wants.
They want to do things to have fun.
They want to have things they like.
Food and clothing are needs.
They can be wants, too.

➤ **Look at the pictures.**

Circle the picture of something someone wants.

Draw a line under the picture of things that can be wants and needs.

Unit Project **Tip!**

Draw three needs.
Draw three wants.
Keep the paper for your project.

www.harcourtschoolsupply.com
31
Unit 2, Chapter 3
Core Skills Social Studies 1, SV 9781419034237

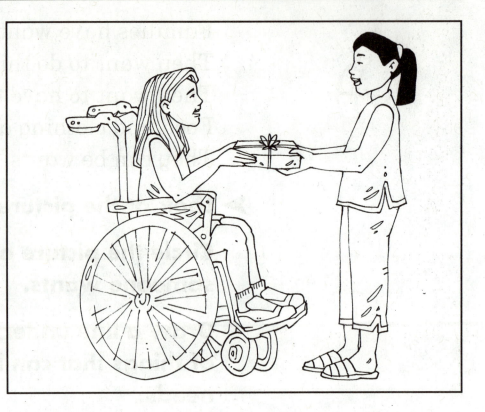

Families need food, clothing, and a place to live.
Families want other things, too.
Look at the picture.
What does it show?

➤ **Make a list of things you need.**

Make a list of things you want.

I need	**I want**
_____	_____
_____	_____
_____	_____
_____	_____

Around the Globe

All Families Need Food

Families live all over the world.
Some families live near us.
Some families live far, far away.
All families, near and far, need food.

➤ **Look at the pictures.**

Put an X on the family eating with their hands.

Draw a line over the family eating with chopsticks.

Circle the people who are shopping for food.

Unit 2, Chapter 3
Core Skills Social Studies 1, SV 9781419034237

Reading a List

Chapter Activity

➤ **You have learned that a list helps you remember things. Look at this list. It lists things Jacob wants and needs.**

Wants	**Needs**
ball	lunch
bicycle	coat
	shoes
_____	_____
....	....
_____	_____

➤ **Answer the questions.**

1. Is lunch a need or a want? Circle the answer.

   need   want

2. Is a bicycle a need or a want? Circle the answer.

   need   want

3. Is a coat a need or a want? Circle the answer.

   need   want

4. Has Jacob listed more needs or more wants? Circle the answer.

   needs   wants

5. Jacob also wants a pet. Write the word **pet** on the correct list above.

Chapter Checkup ✔

➤ **Write an <u>N</u> on things we need.**

 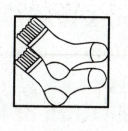  

➤ **Circle the places where people live.**

Thinking & Writing

Is a new bike a need or a want?

Write your answer here.

_____

_____

_____

www.harcourtschoolsupply.com

35

Unit 2, Chapter 3
Core Skills Social Studies 1, SV 9781419034237

CHAPTER 4 — Families at Work

Families work.
Families work to earn money.
They use money to buy things they
need and want.
Some people work at home.
Look at the two pictures.

➤ **Put a ✔ on the picture of the carpenter.**

Draw a line under the picture of the writer.

People work away from home.
Some work in a store.
Some work in a factory.

➤ **Look at the picture.**

Is this a store or a factory?

Circle the answer.

store   **factory**

What do people do in a factory?

➤ **Circle the answer.**

**They make
things.**   **They sell
things.**

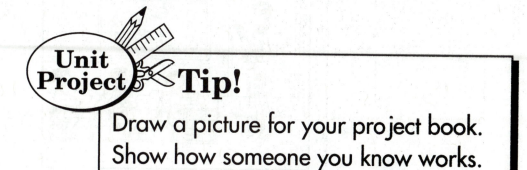

**Unit
Project**

Tip!

Draw a picture for your project book.
Show how someone you know works.

People work to help us.
Some work to keep us safe.
Some work to help us learn.

➤ **Look at the pictures.**

Who helps us learn in school?

Circle two pictures.

Who works to keep us safe?

Draw a line under one picture.

Children can earn money, too.
They can do jobs for family and
neighbors.
All people can earn money.
Then they can buy things they need
and want.
Look at the pictures.
What work are the children doing?
What kinds of work can children do?

➤ **What work would you like to do?**

Write your answer here.

_____

- - - - - - - - - - - - - - - - - - - -

_____

Core Skills Social Studies 1, SV 9781419034237

Special People

Clara Barton

Clara Barton lived long ago.
She was a nurse.
She worked to help sick people.
She started the American Red Cross.
The Red Cross helps people around
the world.
It helps people hurt by big storms
and floods.
Today, men and women are nurses.
Do you know a nurse?

➤ **Draw a picture of a nurse who has
helped you.**

Draw your picture here.

Chapter Activity

Making a Picture List

➤ **Look at the four pictures below. Which jobs can children do? Write the number of each of the jobs children can do in the boxes on the right.**

Jobs Children Can Do

1

2

3

4

Date _____

Chapter Checkup ✓

➤ **Read each question.**

Find a picture it matches.

Write the number in the box above the correct picture.

1. Who helps at home?

2. Who helps us learn to do things?

☐   ☐

Thinking & Writing

Name one worker who keeps us healthy.

Name one worker who helps us learn something.

Write your answers on the lines.

_____

_____

_____

_____

CHAPTER 5 Families Make Choices

Families choose the things they need.
They choose a home.

➤ **Look at the picture.**

Is this a good place for a family?

Why or why not?

Write your answer here.

_____

_____

_____

_____

_____

_____

_____

Unit 2, Chapter 5
Core Skills Social Studies 1, SV 9781419034237

Some families choose to live in tall buildings.
The buildings have room for many families.
Other families choose to live in houses.

➤ **Look at the picture.**

Who lives here?

Circle the answer.

one family   many families

Families need and want many things.
Some families need cars.
How do they choose a car?

➤ **Circle the car that this family should choose.**

Unit Project ✏️📏✂️ **Tip!**

Find or draw more pictures for your book.
Show some homes people choose.

Families want many things.
They cannot have everything they want.

➤ **Why not?**

Write your answer here.

_____

- - - - - - - - - - - - - - - - - - -

_____

_____

- - - - - - - - - - - - - - - - - - -

_____

Chapter Activity

Putting Things in Order

➤ **Ann's mother needs a new car. Read the sentences. They tell what she does to get a car.**

☐ Ann's mother drives her new car home.

☐ Ann's mother goes to look at new cars.

☐ Ann's mother buys the car.

☐ Ann's mother chooses a new car.

1. What does Ann's mother do first? Write a **1** in the box next to the sentence.

2. What does Ann's mother do next? Write a **2** in the box next to the sentence.

3. What does Ann's mother do after that? Write a **3** in the box next to the sentence.

4. What does Ann's mother do last? Write a **4** in the box next to the sentence.

Chapter Checkup ✔

A family must choose the things
it needs.
A family needs a place to live.

➤ **Look at the pictures.**

What does the family choose?

Circle the answer.

A family needs food.

What do they choose?

Put an X on the food they need.

Why must a family choose what to buy?

Write your answer here.

_____

_____

_____

Unit 2 📋 Skill Builder

Making a List

➤ **Find two pictures that show needs.**

Write them on the NEEDS list.

Find two pictures that show wants.

Write them on the WANTS list.

Think of one more want and one more need.

Add their names to your lists.

NEEDS	WANTS
1. _____	1. _____
2. _____	2. _____
3. _____	3. _____

Present Your Project

Now it's time to present your project.
Answer these questions.

- **What are needs?**

- **What are wants?**

- **How do people get money for needs and wants?**

- **How do people choose what to buy?**

Try one of these ideas.

- Put your pictures together in a book. Ask an adult to help you tie the pages together. Make a cover. Put your name on it. Show your book to your family and friends.

- Put your pictures together. Place them on big pieces of colored paper. Tell about your pictures. Put them on a bulletin board.

Unit 2 Test

➤ **Read each question.**

Circle the correct answer.

1. What do all families need?

pets   food   bicycles

2. Which of these is a want?

clothes   dog   food

3. What need keeps a family warm and dry?

food   a home   a store

4. What work do people do in a factory?

buy things   make things   sell things

5. Which of these is a need?

birthday cake   TV   clothes

Thinking & Writing

What are two reasons people work?

Write your answers here.

_____

_____

_____

_____

_____

Unit 3

Where We Live, Work, and Play

People live in all kinds of places.
Think about the place where you live.
- Are there homes for many people?
- Are there places to work and play?

Unit Project

Make a scrapbook about your neighborhood.
Find or make stories and pictures.

Core Skills Social Studies 1, SV 9781419034237

CHAPTER 6 · Your School

We go to school.
It is a place to work and play.
We learn many things in school.

➤ **Read the sentences below.**

Circle the sentences that tell what you do in school.

I play with friends.

I learn to read and write.

I sleep.

I learn to share.

I work with my teacher.

Here is a picture of a classroom.
This is where we work in school.

➤ **Find the right side of the classroom.**

What is on top of the table?
Circle the answer.

rabbit   paints   ball

➤ **Find the left side of the classroom.**

What is on the wall?

rabbit   books   window

This is a picture of the same classroom.

➤ **What is near the teacher's desk?**

Write your answer here.

_____

- -

_____

➤ **Find the flag.**

What do you see next to the flag?

Write your answer here.

_____

- -

_____

We have rules in school.
Rules tell us what to do.
Rules tell us what not to do.
Read the rules.

1. We work quietly.

2. We give other people a turn.

➤ **Now look at the pictures.**

Match each rule to the correct picture.

Write the number of each rule in the correct box.

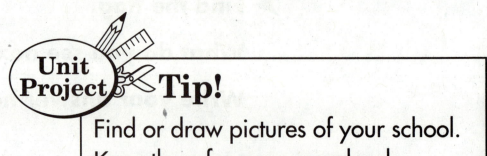

Unit Project **Tip!**

Find or draw pictures of your school.
Keep them for your scrapbook.

We need rules.
Rules help us live together.
Rules help keep us safe.
Rules make things fair.

➤ **Look at the picture.**

What rule is the girl breaking?

_____

- - - - - - - - - - - - - - - - - -

_____

- - - - - - - - - - - - - - - - - -

_____

➤ **Which rule helps you the most? Why?**

_____

- - - - - - - - - - - - - - - - - -

_____

_____

- - - - - - - - - - - - - - - - - -

_____

Most schools have a playground.
This is where you play at school.
Look at the picture of this playground.
There are trees and slides.

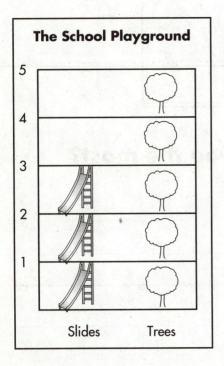

The School Playground

Slides   Trees

Look at the **picture graph**.
The picture graph shows how **many**.

► **How many trees are
on the picture graph?
Write your answer here.** _____

**How many slides
do you see?
Write your answer here.** _____

Who helps us at school?
The librarian helps us find books.
The teacher helps us learn to read them.

➤ **Look at the pictures.**

Who is helping?

Write the answer next to each picture.

_____

- -

_____

- -

Children Go to School

Children go to school all over the world.
In Mexico, people speak Spanish.
The Spanish word for school is **escuela**.
Mexican children go to an **escuela** to learn.
Look at the picture.
Does the school in Mexico look like your school?

➤ **Draw a picture of your school here.**

Learning About Rules

Chapter Activity

Rules tell us what to do and not do. Families have safety, clean-up, and bedtime rules.

WORD BOX
safety clean-up bedtime

➤ **Look at the four pictures below. One picture does not show a rule. Mark an X on it.**

Three pictures show rules. Write the word from the box that tells the kind of rule each of the pictures shows.

_____

_____

_____

_____

_____

_____

Reading a Picture Graph

Chapter Activity

➤ **Look at this picture graph. It shows how many children are in the first grade class.**

The First Grade Class

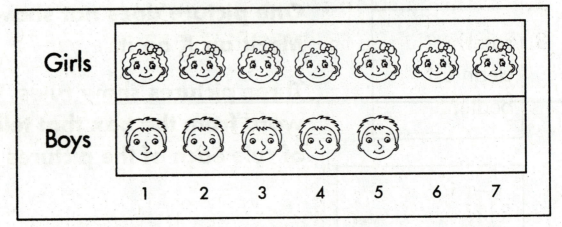

Girls

Boys

1 2 3 4 5 6 7

1. Find the name of the graph.
Draw a line under it.

2. How many boys are in the first grade class?
Write your answer here.

_____

- -

_____

3. Are there more boys or girls?
Write your answer here.

_____

- -

_____

Chapter Checkup ✔

➤ **Some words tell where things are. Read the sentences. Then cut out the pictures at the bottom. Paste them where they go in the picture.**

1. Put the teacher's desk **in front of** the board.

2. Put the globe **on top of** the teacher's desk.

3. Put the flag on the **left side** of the classroom.

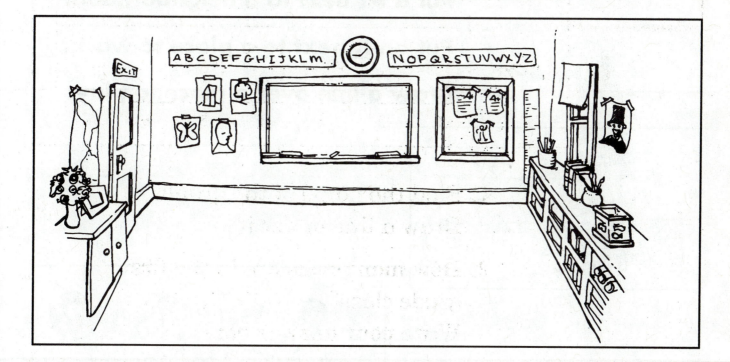

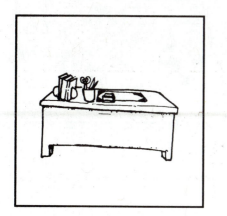

CHAPTER 7 — Families Live in Neighborhoods

What is a **neighborhood**?
It is where families live.
It is where families work and play.

➤ **Look at the pictures.**

Put a ✔ next to a neighborhood.

Put an X next to a place to work.

Draw a line over a place to play.

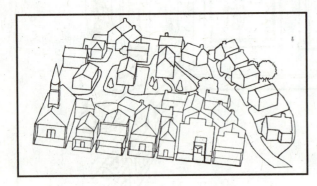

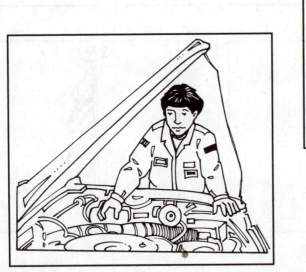

There are many kinds of neighborhoods.
Some neighborhoods are in the city.
Some are in the country.

➤ **Look at the two pictures.**

How are these neighborhoods alike?

_____

- -

_____

_____

- -

_____

_____

- -

_____

_____

- -

_____

Look at the picture on these two pages.
It is a picture of a neighborhood.
There are places to live, work, and play.
What places can you find?

➤ **Find a place to play.**

Circle it.

Find a place to buy food.
Draw a line under it.

Find a place where many people can live.

Put a ✔ next to it.

A **map** of another neighborhood is on the next page.

A map is a special drawing of a place. The **map key** tells what the pictures on the map mean.

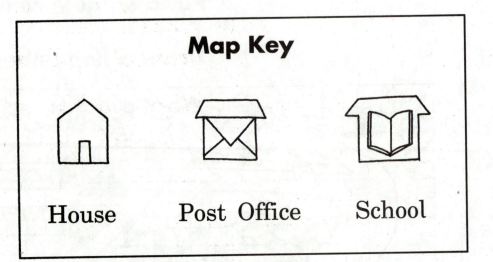

Map Key

House   Post Office   School

➤ **Look at the map key above.**

Find the picture for <u>House</u>.

Put a ✔ under it.

Find the picture for <u>School</u>.

Draw a line under it.

Find the arrows on the map. These arrows show **directions**. Directions show the way to go. North, south, east, and west are directions.

➤ **What is west of Center Street? Draw a line under it.**

What place is east of the art museum? Circle it.

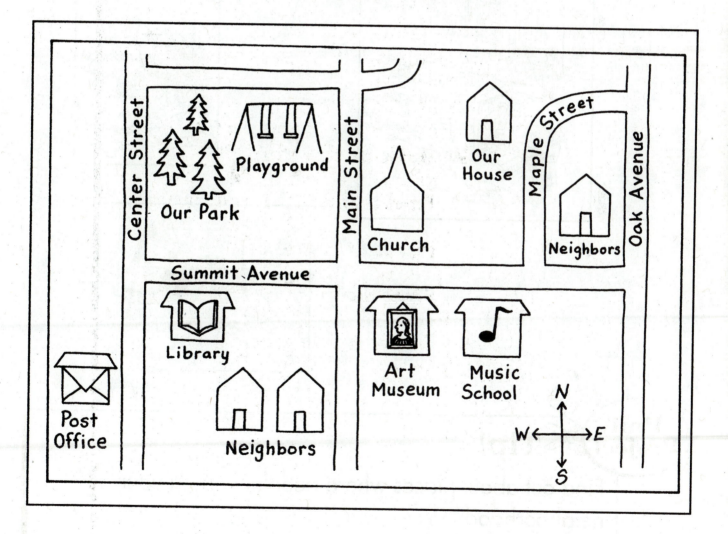

These pictures show how neighborhoods change.

➤ **Which family is moving?**

Put a red ✔ next to the picture.

Who is planting a garden?

Draw a line under the picture.

Unit Project Tip!

Find out about places where people work in your neighborhood.
Write about what people do there.

Benjamin Franklin

Benjamin Franklin lived long, long ago.
He lived in the city of Philadelphia.
There was no hospital for sick people.
There was no library to get books.
Mr. Franklin helped build a hospital and library.
He helped many, many families.

➤ **Do you use the library?**

Draw a map of your library here.

Draw a map key, too.

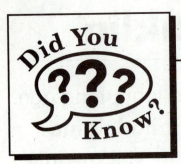

Places from Long Ago

Long ago, families built their own homes.
They built places to work, too.
Today, you can visit some of these places.
You can see how families lived long ago.
You can learn how families and places have changed.
You can learn how families and places have stayed the same.

➤ **Look at the picture.**

What would you ask someone who lived here long ago?

Write your question here.

_____

_____

_____

_____

Unit 3, Chapter 7
Core Skills Social Studies 1, SV 9781419034237

Name _____   Date _____

Finishing a Map

➤ **Look at the top picture of a library. Below it, a map of the library has been started. Finish the map. Draw the missing things on the map.**

Chapter Checkup ✔

➤ **Read the words in the box.**

Write each word next to the correct picture.

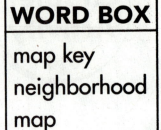

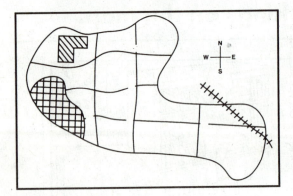

_____

- - - - - - - - - - - - - - - - - - - -

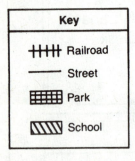

_____

- - - - - - - - - - - - - - - - - - - -

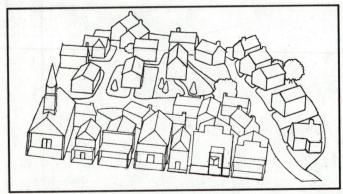

_____

- - - - - - - - - - - - - - - - - - - -

In what ways can a neighborhood change?

Write your answer here.

_____

- - - - - - - - - - - - - - - - - - - -

_____

Unit 3 📋 Skill Builder

Using a Map Key

Remember that a map is a special drawing of a place. Look at the map and map key.

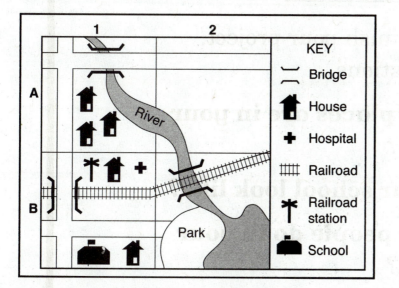

1. Find the park on the map.
   Color it green.

2. Find the school on the map.
   Put a blue **X** on the school.

3. How many houses are in the neighborhood?
   Write your answer here.

_____

_____

_____

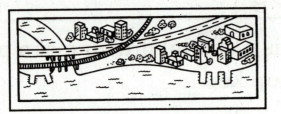

Present Your Project

Now it is time to finish your project. Answer these questions.

- **What kinds of places are in your neighborhood?**

- **What does your school look like?**

- **What work do people do in your neighborhood?**

Try one of these ideas.

- Put your pictures together. Make a scrapbook of your neighborhood. Add stories that tell about the places.

- Tell your family and friends about your neighborhood. Show the pictures of your neighborhood.

- Tell a story about one picture.

Unit 3 ✏ Test

➤ **Read the words in the box.**

Write each word next to the correct picture.

WORD BOX

map key
directions
a school rule

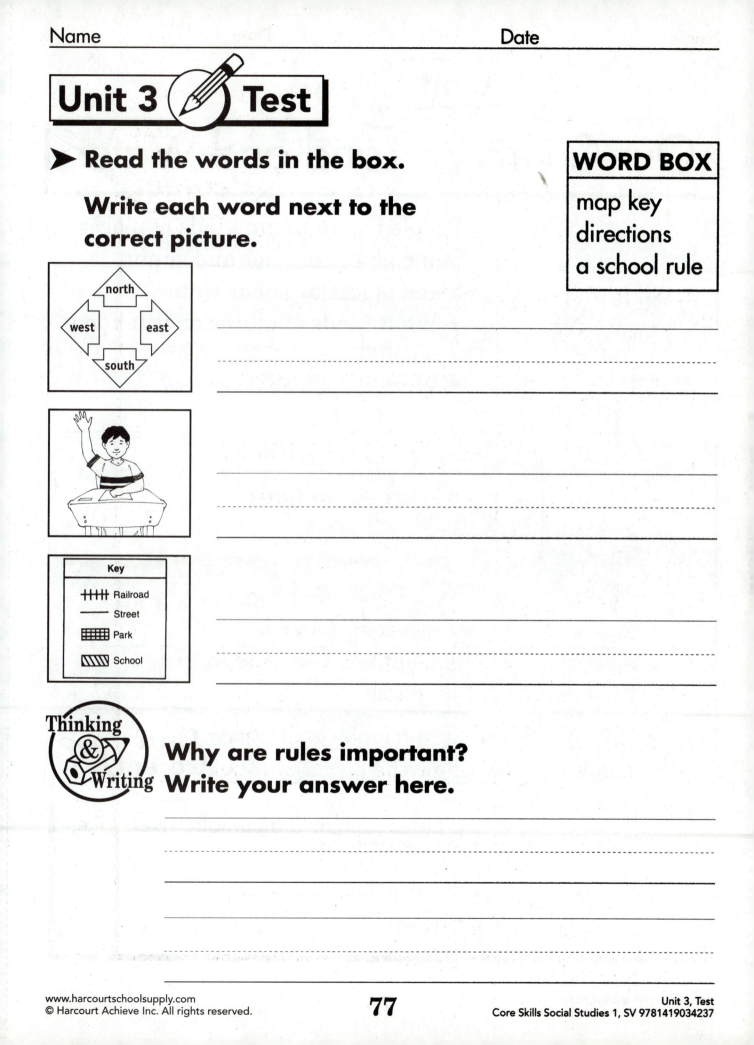

Thinking & Writing

Why are rules important?
Write your answer here.

Unit 4
Our Country's Land and Water

People live in many kinds of places.
Some places are hot and sunny.
Some places are near water.

- What kinds of places do you know about?
- What do people do there?

Unit Project

Pick a place such as a mountain, river, lake, or another place you know about.
Find out why the place is special.
Make a book or model of the place.

Families Live in Different Places

We live on **Earth**.
Color the water blue.
Color the land green.

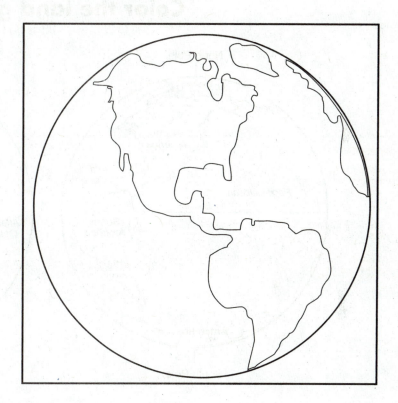

Earth is not flat.
It is round like a ball.

➤ **Can you see all sides of Earth at one time?**

Circle the answer.

yes   **no**

These are pictures of a **globe**.
A globe is round like Earth.
But a globe is much, much smaller.
You can hold a globe in your hands.
You can see water and land on a globe.

➤ **Color the water blue.**

Color the land green.

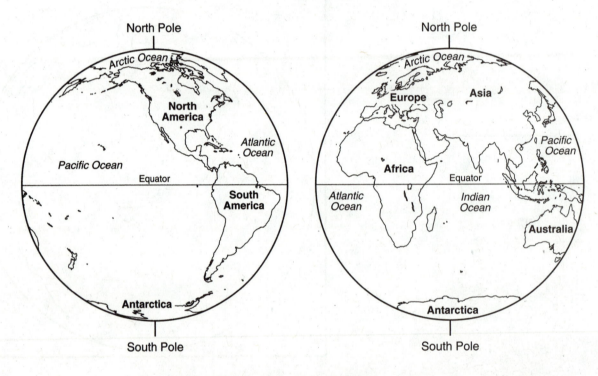

➤ **Find North America on the globe.**

Circle North America.

Unit Project ✂ **Tip!**

Look at pictures in books of the place you chose.
Draw pictures of what the place looks like.
What plants, animals, and people live there?

Earth is very big.
Families live in many places.
Some families live on farms.
These farms are on flat land.
Other families live near **mountains**.
A mountain is very high land.

➤ **Look at the pictures.**

Put a red ✔ below the farm.

Put a green ✔ below the mountains.

Some families live near water.
They may live near **rivers**.
A river is water that flows across
the land.
What is the place like where you live?
Is the land flat, or is it high?
Is there water where you live?

➤ **Draw a picture of where you live.**

Draw your picture here.

People work in many places.
Some people work on the water.
Some people work high in the air.
Where would you like to work?

➤ **Look at the pictures.**

Who is working on the water?
Put a red ✔ below the picture.

Who works high in the air?
Put a blue ✔ below the picture.

Around the Globe

People at Work

People work all over the world.
Look at the picture of the farmer.
He is working in a field of wheat.

➤ **Circle what the man is growing.**

➤ **Read the sentences below.**

Circle the sentence that tells about the picture.

The farm is on flat land.

The farm is on a mountain.

The farm is on a beach.

Chapter Activity

Understanding a Globe

➤ **Remember that a globe looks like Earth. It shows the land and water on Earth. Look at this picture of a globe.**

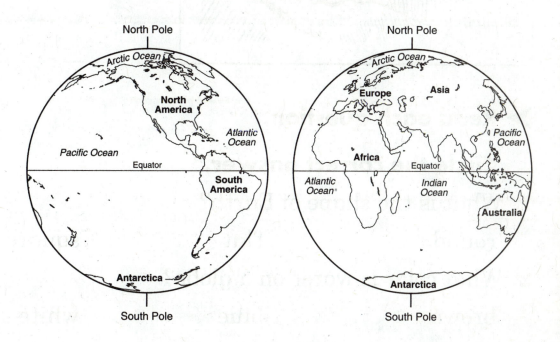

1. Color the land green.

2. Color the water blue.

3. What shape is the globe?

_____

_____

4. Is there more water or land on Earth?

_____

_____

Chapter Checkup ✔

➤ **Read each question.**

Circle the correct answer.

1. What is the shape of Earth?

   round   flat   square

2. What color is water on a globe?

   brown   blue   white

3. Which can you hold in your hand?

   globe   Earth   mountain

4. What is the place like where you live?

   in the mountains   on flat land   near water

Thinking & Writing

Why are most farms on flat land and not mountains?

_____

_____

_____

CHAPTER 9 Taking Care of Our Resources

The United States has many **resources**.

Resources are things found on Earth.

They are things like land, trees, and water.

Even air is a resource.

➤ **Look at the picture.**

Tell what resources are in the picture.

Write your answer below the picture.

_____

- -

_____

- -

_____

- -

_____

Resources are in all parts of the United States.

➤ **Look at the map of the United States.**

In what part of the United States do you live?

Put an X near where you live.

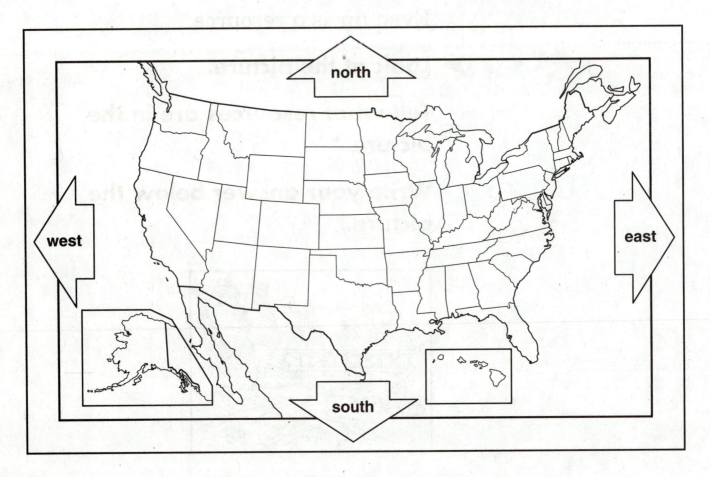

1

People cannot make resources.
So we must take care of them.
Plants, animals, and clean air are
resources all people use.
The pictures show some resources.
Show where we find them.
Use the map on page 88.

2

► **Picture 1 shows large trees.
These trees grow in the West.
Put a red ✔ in the West on
the map.**

**Picture 2 shows clean water
in a river.
This river is in the South.
Put a blue ✔ in the South on
the map.**

3

**Picture 3 shows good land for
farming.
This land is in the North.
Put a green ✔ in the North
on the map.**

We need clean water, land, and air.
Pollution makes water, land, and
air dirty.
Pollution hurts living things.
Pollution hurts our resources.

➤ **Put a red ✔ next to clean
resources.**

**Put a blue ✔ next to a picture of
pollution.**

Core Skills Social Studies 1, SV 9781419034237

How can we stop pollution?
We can stop making more pollution.
We can pick up cans.
We can throw things we do not want into a basket.
We can ask others to help.
People around the world can help.

➤ **Make a sign.**
Tell people to help stop pollution.

Draw your sign here.

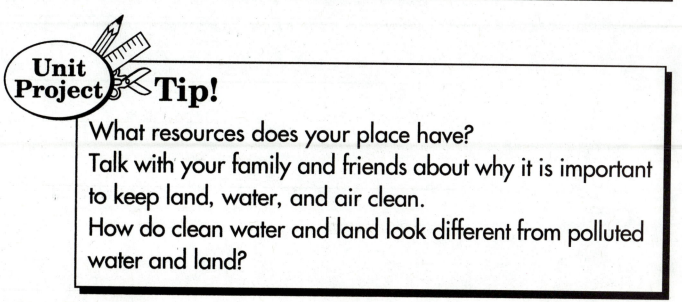

Unit Project Tip!

What resources does your place have?
Talk with your family and friends about why it is important to keep land, water, and air clean.
How do clean water and land look different from polluted water and land?

Name _____   Date _____

Special People

Theodore Roosevelt

Theodore Roosevelt was the 26th President of the United States a long time ago.

He cared about our resources.

He made places safe for birds and other animals to live.

Mr. Roosevelt also started big parks around the United States.

Many people visit these parks every year.

➤ **What can you do to keep our resources safe?**

Write your answers here.

_____

_____

_____

_____

_____

_____

Unit 4, Chapter 9
Core Skills Social Studies 1, SV 9781419034237

Chapter Activity

Working with a Resource Map

➤ **Look at the map. This map shows some of the resources of the United States. Read the sentences. Do what they tell you to do.**

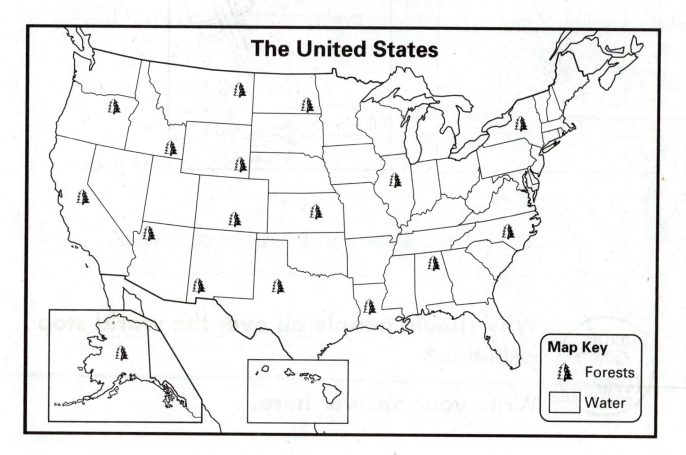

The United States

Map Key

🌲 Forests

▢ Water

1. Find the forests. Color all the trees green.

2. Find the water. Fish live in water.
They are an important resource, too.
Draw pictures of fish in the water.

3. Color all the water blue.

Chapter Checkup ✔

➤ **Look at the pictures.**
Write the name of each
resource below.
Use two words from the box.

_____   _____

Why should people all over the world stop pollution?

Write your answer here.

_____

_____

_____

_____

Unit 4 📋 Skill Builder

Using a United States Map

➤ **Look at the map of the United States.**

1. Circle the arrow that points North.

2. Color the land brown.

3. Color one state in the South green.

4. Color all the water blue.

5. Draw a tree in the West.

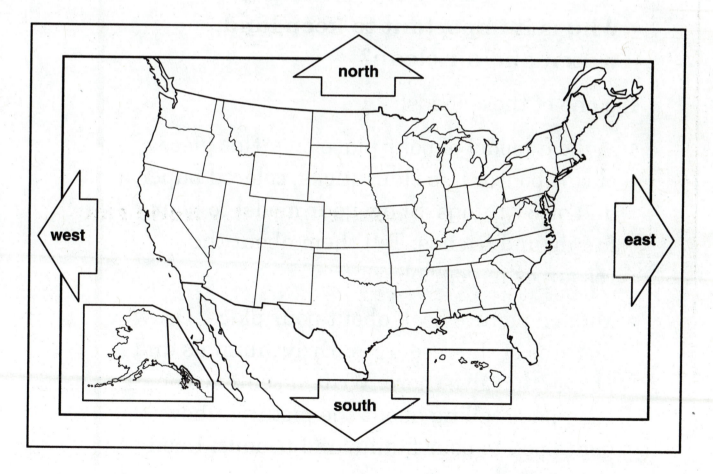

Present Your Project

Now it is time to finish your project.

Answer these questions.

- **What plants, animals, and people live in the place you chose?**

- **What resources does your place have?**

- **Why is it important to keep land, water, and air clean?**

Try one of these ideas.

- Make a model of your place on a flat piece of cardboard. Use clay, sticks, colored paper, and other things. Show your model to your family and friends. Tell them about the resources in your place.

- Make a picture book about your place. Draw pictures of the resources. Draw animals and people that live there. Write a sentence on each page telling about the picture. Show your book to your family and friends. Read the sentences out loud.

Name _____ Date _____

Unit 4  Test

➤ **Read each question.**
  Circle the correct answer.

1. What is the name of the place where we live?
  Earth   globe

2. Where do most farmers plant corn?
  in the mountains   on flat land

3. What are land, water, and air?
  pollution   resources

4. What makes the air dirty?
  pollution   farming

5. Can we stop pollution?
  yes   no

 **What will happen if we do not take care of our resources?**

Write your answer here.

_____
- -
_____
- -
_____

Unit 5
Families Long Ago and Today

The first Americans were American Indians.

They came to America long, long ago.

- How did American Indian families find homes, food, and clothing?
- How did American Indians help other families who came to America?
- How do families share holidays?

Unit Project

Learn about a holiday that families share.

Find or draw pictures about the holiday.

Find out what people do on the holiday.

CHAPTER 10 First American Families

Many American Indians live in the
United States.
They have lived in the United States
for a long, long time.
They built homes and made clothes.
They hunted and fished for food.
They showed their children many
things.

Look at the picture.
The girl is learning to make cloth.

➤**Who is teaching the girl?**

Write your answer here.

_____

_____

How did American Indians live long ago?

There were no stores then.

They grew food.

They hunted and fished.

Some made clothing from the skins of animals.

➤ **Find the picture of the American Indian growing food.**

Put a ✔ on the picture.

Find the American Indian hunting.
Put an X on the picture.

Look at the picture of an American Indian village.
These American Indians lived in homes called **tepees**.

➤ **Put an X on the tepees that are far away.**

Put a ✔ on the tepee that is on the far left.

 **Unit Project** ✂ **Tip!**

Long ago, American Indians shared one holiday with some new Americans.
You will find out about this holiday.
Do you know what it is?

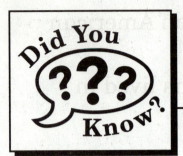

American Indian Homes

American Indians lived in all parts of the United States. They had different kinds of homes.

They made their homes from things they found where they lived.

Some families made homes of wood.

Some families made homes of grass.

Other families made homes of animal skins.

➤ **Pretend it is long ago.**

What is your home made of?

Draw a picture of what your home might look like.

Learning from a Picture

➤ **Look at the picture of the American Indian home. Read the sentences. Do what they tell you to do.**

1. Circle what is **near** the river.

2. Put a ✔ on what is **far** from the river.

3. Is the horse pen on the **right** side or the **left** side of the house?

_____

- -

_____

Chapter Checkup ✓

➤ **Read the sentences below.**

Circle the sentences that are true.

The first Americans were American Indians.

Long, long ago, American Indians bought their food in stores.

American Indians made their clothes.

American Indians hunted animals for food.

Some American Indians farmed.

All American Indians lived in tepees.

How is an American Indian family of long ago like your family?

Write your answer here.

_____

_____

_____

_____

CHAPTER 11 Families and the First Thanksgiving

Long ago, the Pilgrims came to America.
They grew food.
They hunted and fished.
American Indians helped the Pilgrims.
The Pilgrims and American Indians
shared the first Thanksgiving.

➤ **Look at the picture.**

What is one thing that is happening?

Write your answer here.

_____

_____

_____

_____

Today, families still share
Thanksgiving.
Thanksgiving is in November.
Some families have big, big dinners.
They eat special foods.
They have friends visit.

What does your family do on Thanksgiving?

Write about your Thanksgiving here.

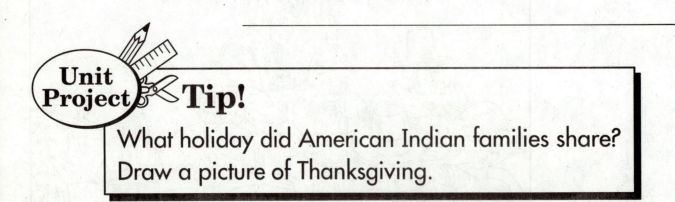

Unit Project

Tip!

What holiday did American Indian families share?
Draw a picture of Thanksgiving.

Look at the **chart** below.
A chart has facts in order.
The facts are listed in a table.
This chart tells about the first
Thanksgiving.
It also tells about Thanksgiving today.

	First Thanksgiving	**Thanksgiving Today**
People	Pilgrims and American Indians	friends and family
Food	hunted for turkey	buy turkey in store
Time	three days	one day

➤ **Read the chart.**
   How long was the first Thanksgiving?
   Write your answer here.

_____

_____

➤ **Where do people get turkeys today?**
   Write your answer here.

_____

_____

_____

Special People

Squanto

Squanto was an American Indian.
He lived long ago.
He helped the Pilgrims.
The Pilgrims were new to America.
They did not know how to live here.
Squanto showed the Pilgrims how to grow corn.
He showed them how to catch fish.
He helped them get syrup from trees.

➤ **What would have happened to the Pilgrims without Squanto's help?**

Write your answer here.

_____

_____

_____

_____

➤ **Draw a picture of Squanto helping the Pilgrims. Use another sheet of paper.**

Chapter Activity

Reading a Chart

➤ **Remember that a chart gives facts in order. This chart gives facts about Squanto. Look at the chart. Then answer the questions.**

Squanto	
Year he was born	about 1585
American Indian group	Patuxet
Where he lived	near Plymouth Colony

1. What is the name of the chart?

_____

- -

_____

2. Squanto was a member of an American Indian group. What was the name of the group?

_____

- -

_____

3. Where did Squanto live?

_____

- -

_____

www.harcourtschoolsupply.com   **109**   Unit 5, Chapter 11
               Core Skills Social Studies 1, SV 9781419034237

Chapter Checkup ✔

➤ **Read the sentences. Circle the sentences that are true.**

Thanksgiving is in April.

Squanto helped the Pilgrims.

Today, Thanksgiving lasts three days.

The Pilgrims hunted their turkeys.

Pilgrims and American Indians shared the first
Thanksgiving.

**Why did the Pilgrims share Thanksgiving
with the American Indians?**

Write your answer here.

_____

_____

_____

_____

_____

_____

_____

CHAPTER 12 Ways We Celebrate and Remember

Families get together on special days called **holidays**.

Families **celebrate** on these days.

Celebrate means to remember a special day.

Some families celebrate Christmas. They trim a tree.

Some families celebrate Hanukkah. They light candles.

Some families celebrate Kwanzaa. They light candles, too.

➤ **What is one holiday that your family celebrates? Write the name here.**

_____

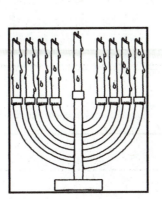

Look at the parade!
It is the Fourth of July.
It is the birthday of the United States.
Do you see the flag in the picture?
It is the flag of the United States.

➤ **Does your family celebrate the Fourth of July? If so, what do you do?**

_____

_____

_____

_____

The flag stands for the United States.

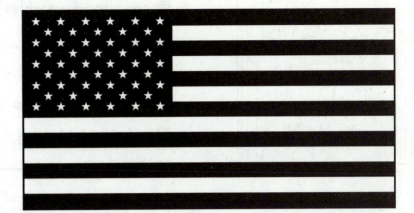

Look at the flag.
There are 50 stars on the flag.
The dark stripes are red.
The light stripes are white.

➤ **How many red stripes are on the flag?**

Write your answer here.

_____

- - - - - - - - - - - - - - - - - -

_____

How many white stripes are on the flag?

Write your answer here.

_____

- - - - - - - - - - - - - - - - - -

_____

          Core Skills Social Studies 1, SV 9781419034237

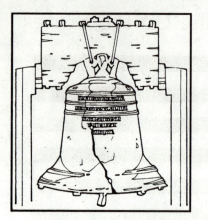

This is the Liberty Bell.
It makes us think of the United
States, too.
The Liberty Bell is over 200 years old.
It is in the city of Philadelphia.
Philadelphia is in the state of
Pennsylvania.

➤ **Look around your neighborhood.**

**What do you see that makes you
think of the United States?**

Write your answer here.

_____

- -

_____

Unit Project **Tip!**

What are some things people do to
celebrate the Fourth of July?
Find or draw pictures of this holiday.
How do you celebrate this holiday?

114

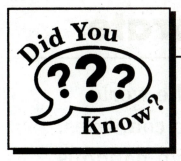

Caring for the Flag

We must take care of the flag.
There is a special way.
Match each sentence to the correct picture.

1. We raise the flag.

2. We salute the flag.

3. We fold the flag.

Families Celebrate

Families live all over the world.
Families love their own countries.
They celebrate their own holidays.

➤ **What are some holidays your family celebrates?**

Make a list here.

_____

- -

_____

_____

- -

_____

_____

- -

_____

Reading a Chart

➤ **This chart shows holidays in other countries. Look at the chart. Then answer the questions.**

Holidays in Other Countries

Holiday	Country	Month
Arbor Day	Spain	March
African Freedom Day	Chad	May
Cinco de Mayo	Mexico	May
Respect for the Aged Day	Japan	September

1. When is Respect for the Aged Day celebrated?

_____

- -

_____

2. Which country celebrates African Freedom Day?

_____

- -

_____

3. What holiday is celebrated in March?

_____

- -

_____

4. When does Mexico celebrate Cinco de Mayo?

_____

- -

_____

Chapter Checkup

➤ Read the sentences. Do what they tell you to do.

1. Circle the colors of the United States flag.

  red green white blue

2. What is the birthday of the United States?
   Circle the correct answer.

  Fourth of July Christmas Hanukkah

3. Do families all over the world celebrate holidays?
   Circle the correct answer.

  yes no

4. What do you think of when you see the flag?
   Write your answer here.

_____

- -

_____

What are two ways families celebrate holidays?

_____

- -

_____

- -

_____

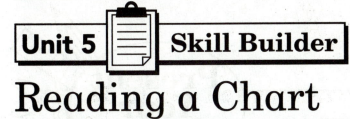

Unit 5 | Skill Builder

Reading a Chart

A chart lists facts in a table.
Look at the chart.

Some United States Holidays		
Holiday	**What is celebrated**	**Month it is celebrated**
President's Day	Birthdays of two U.S. Presidents	February
Flag Day	United States flag	June
Earth Day	Land, water, and air on Earth	April

➤ **Answer each question on the lines.**

1. When is Earth Day celebrated?

_____

_____

2. What holiday is celebrated in February?

_____

_____

3. What holiday could you add to the chart?

_____

_____

Present Your Project

Now it is time to finish your project. Answer these questions.

- **What holiday did American Indians share with other Americans?**

- **Do all families celebrate the same holidays?**

- **How do people celebrate holidays?**

- **What are some holidays you know about?**

Try one of these ideas.

- Make pictures of the holiday you chose. Show how families celebrate the holiday. Draw pictures of special foods they eat. Make models of the special things used to celebrate the holiday.

- Put your pictures in a book. Tell your family and friends about the holiday. Show them your pictures. Tell them what people do.

Unit 5 ✎ Test

➤ **Read each sentence.**
Circle the sentences that are true.

1. The first Americans were Pilgrims.

2. American Indians grew some of their food.

3. The Pilgrims celebrated the first Kwanzaa.

4. Squanto helped the Pilgrims make clothes from the skins of animals.

5. The Liberty Bell can make us think of the United States.

What are two ways families celebrate the Fourth of July?

Write your answer here.

_____

_____

_____

_____

_____

_____

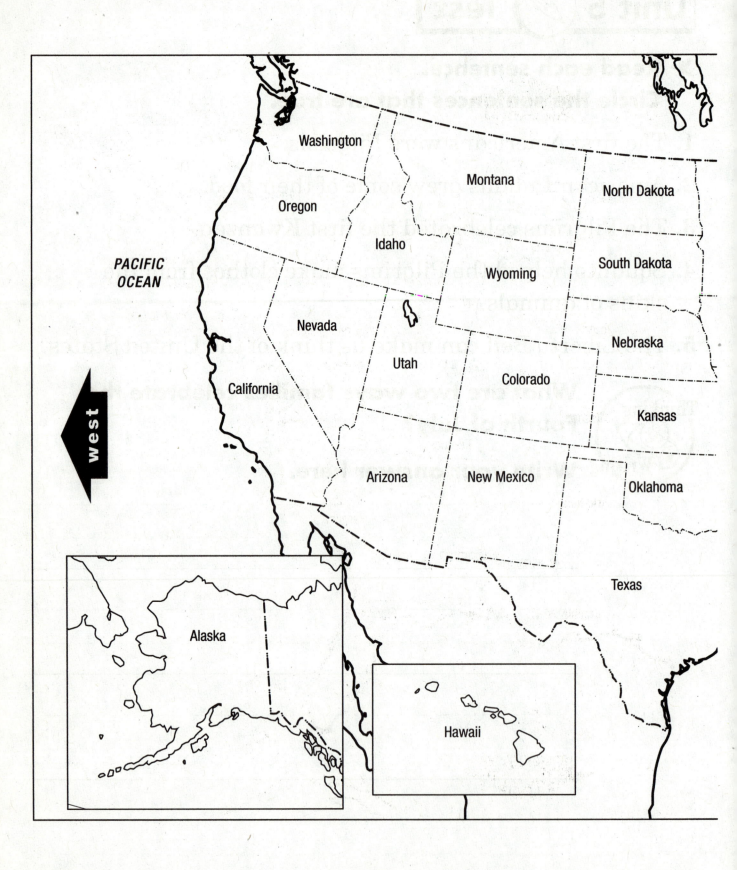

PACIFIC OCEAN

Washington
Oregon
Idaho
Montana
North Dakota
South Dakota
Wyoming
Nevada
Utah
Colorado
Nebraska
California
Kansas
Arizona
New Mexico
Oklahoma
Texas

west

Alaska

Hawaii

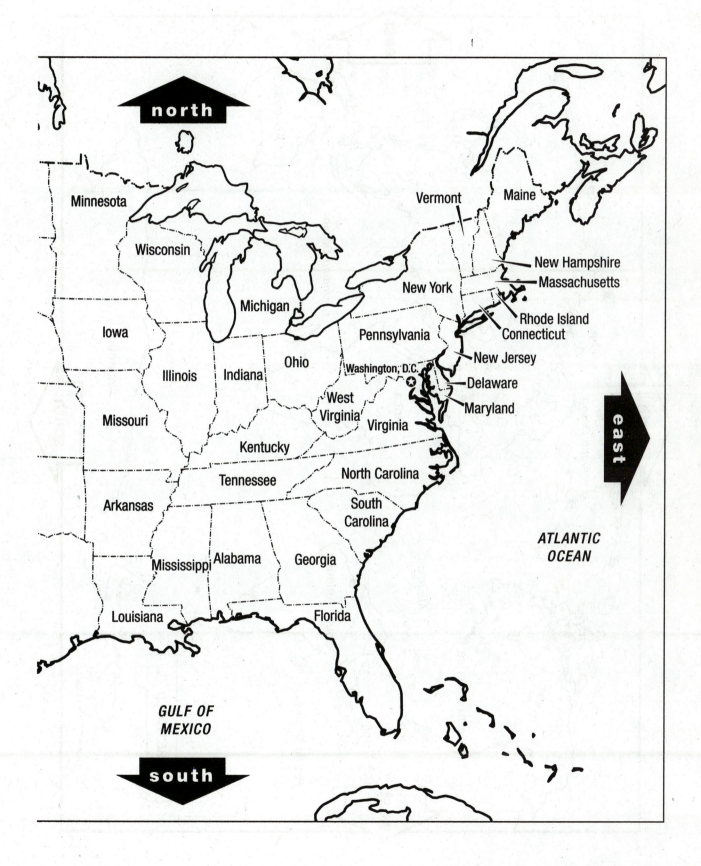

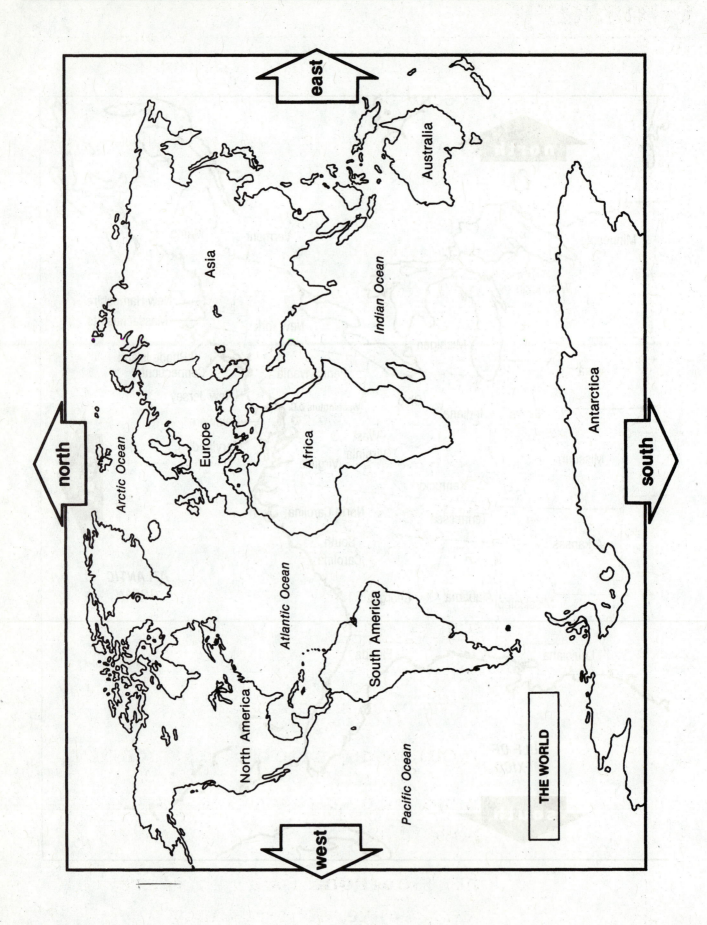

east

north

south

west

Australia

Asia

Indian Ocean

Arctic Ocean

Europe

Africa

Antarctica

Atlantic Ocean

South America

North America

Pacific Ocean

THE WORLD

www.harcourtschoolsupply.com
124
World Map
Core Skills Social Studies 1, SV 9781419034237

Glossary

celebrate (page 111) to remember a special day

chart (page 107) a table that lists facts in order

directions (page 69) a way to go. The directions are north, south, east, and west.

Earth (page 79) the planet we live on

family (page 6) your parents, brothers and sisters, and other relatives

globe (page 80) a round map of Earth

holidays (page 111) special days such as Thanksgiving or the Fourth of July

map (page 68) a special drawing of a place

map key (page 68) tells what the pictures on a map mean

mountains (page 81) very high land

need (page 27) something you must have to live

neighborhood (page 64) where families live, work, and play

picture graph (page 58) a graph that uses pictures to show how many

pollution (page 90) makes land, water, and air dirty

resources (page 87) things found on Earth, such as land, trees, and water

rivers (page 82) water that flows across the land

rules (page 18) instructions that tell what to do and what not to do

tepees (page 101) a kind of home that American Indians lived in

want (page 27) something you would like to have

Glossary
Core Skills Social Studies 1, SV 9781419034237

Answer Key

For answers not provided, check that children have given an appropriate response and/or followed the directions given.

Page 14
Children should correctly number the pictures in this order: top row, left to right should be 2, 4; bottom row, left to right should be 1, 3.

Page 19   Go to bed at a good hour; Brush your teeth.

Page 21
1. Children should draw a line under the two children near the slide.
2. Children should circle the dog that is next to the swings.
3. near   4. far

Page 22   Children should circle the riders who are not following bike safety rules.
Answers will vary.

Page 23
1. Children should circle the two families who are playing.
2. Children should draw a line between the two families who are working. Answers will vary about families' work differences.

Page 25
1. yes   2. no   3. yes   4. yes   5. yes
Answers will vary.

Page 27
Children should circle the food and clothes. Children should check the ice cream cone and the toy.

Page 34
1. need   2. want   3. need   4. needs
5. Children should add *pet* to the list of wants.

Page 35
Children should write an **N** on the house, socks, and milk.
Children should circle the house and apartments.
want

Page 37
Children should circle *factory* and *They make things*.

Page 41   Children should identify pictures 1, 2, and 3 as the jobs children can do.

Page 42   Children should write 1 above the picture on the left and 2 above the picture on the right.
Answers will vary.

Page 44   Children should circle *many families*.

Page 47
The correct order is:
1. Ann's mother goes to look at new cars.   2. Ann's mother chooses a new car.   3. Ann's mother buys the car.   4. Ann's mother drives her new car home.

Page 48
Children should circle the house.
Children should put an *X* on the meal.
Answers will vary.

Page 49
Needs
1. Clothes   2. House   3. Answers will vary.
Wants
1. Sports equipment   2. Pet   3. Answers will vary.

Page 51
1. food   2. dog   3. a home
4. make things   5. clothes
Possible answers: to earn money, to buy needs and wants, to help people, to keep people safe.

Page 53
Children should circle *I play with friends*, *I learn to read and write*, *I learn to share*, and *I work with my teacher*.

Page 54
Children should circle *rabbit*.
Children should circle *window*.

Page 55
Children should write *door*, *chalkboard*, *flag*, or *trash can*.
Children should write *bookcase*, *chalkboard*, *trash can*, or *teacher's desk*.

Page 58   5, 3

Page 61   Children should mark the top picture with an *X*; they should identify the next picture as showing a bedtime rule; the next picture should be identified as a clean-up rule; the bottom picture as a safety rule.

Page 62

1. Children should underline the name of the graph: "The First Grade Class."
2. 5   3. more girls

Page 63

1. Children should cut out the teacher's desk and paste it in front of the board.
2. Children should cut out the globe and paste it on top of the teacher's desk.
3. Children should cut out the flag and paste it on the left side of the classroom.

Page 69

Children should draw a line under the post office.
Children should circle the music school.

Page 73

Children should draw the librarian's desk, the bookcase, and the computer on the map in positions corresponding to their location in the illustration.

Page 74   map, map key, neighborhood

Answers will vary.

Page 75

1. Children should color the park green.
2. Children should place a blue X on the school.
3. 5

Page 77   directions, a school rule, map key

Possible answers: they help people get along; they keep things fair; they keep people safe.

Page 79   no

Page 84   Children should circle *The farm is on flat land.*

Page 85

1. Children should color the land green.
2. Children should color the water blue.
3. round   4. more water

Page 86

1. round   2. blue   3. globe   4. Answers will vary.
Answers will vary.

Page 93

1. Children should color all the trees green.
2. Children should draw fish in the water.
3. Children should color all the water blue.

Page 94   water, land

Answers will vary.

Page 95

1. Children should circle the arrow that points North.
2. Children should color the land brown.
3. Children should color one state in the South green.
4. Children should color all the water blue.
5. Children should draw a tree in the West.

Page 97

1. Earth   2. on flat land   3. resources
4. pollution   5. yes
Possible Answer: We will run out of resources.

Page 103

1. Children should circle the horse pen.
2. Children should put a check mark on the field with crops or vegetables.
3. the left

Page 104   Children should circle: The first Americans were American Indians; American Indians made their clothes; American Indians hunted animals for food; Some American Indians farmed.

Answers will vary.

Page 107   three days, buy turkey in the store

Page 109

1. Squanto   2. Patuxet
3. near Plymouth Colony

Page 110

Children should circle: Squanto helped the Pilgrims; The Pilgrims hunted their turkeys; Pilgrims and American Indians shared the first Thanksgiving.
Answers will vary.

Page 113   7, 6

Page 117

1. September   2. Chad   3. Arbor Day   4. May

Page 118

1. red, white, blue   2. Fourth of July
3. yes   4. Answers will vary.
5. Answers will vary.

Page 119

1. April   2. President's Day   3. Answers will vary.

Page 121

Children should circle the second and fifth sentences.
Possible answers: with parades, fireworks, picnics, putting up a flag.

Answer Key
Core Skills Social Studies 1, SV 9781419034237